Once Upon A Dream

Imaginary Realms

Edited By Lynsey Evans

First published in Great Britain in 2024 by:

Young Writers
Remus House
Coltsfoot Drive
Peterborough
PE2 9BF
Telephone: 01733 890066
Website: www.youngwriters.co.uk

Book Design by Ashley Janson

Softback ISBN 978-1-83565-415-6
Printed and bound in the UK by BookPrintingUK
Website: www.bookprintinguk.com
YB0589O

FOREWORD

Welcome Reader, to a world of dreams.

For Young Writers' latest competition, we asked our writers to dig deep into their imagination and create a poem that paints a picture of what they dream of, whether it's a make-believe world full of wonder or their aspirations for the future.

The result is this collection of fantastic poetic verse that covers a whole host of different topics. Let your mind fly away with the fairies to explore the sweet joy of candy lands, join in with a game of fantasy football, or you may even catch a glimpse of a unicorn or another mythical creature. Beware though, because even dreamland has dark corners, so you may turn a page and walk into a nightmare!

Whereas the majority of our writers chose to stick to a free verse style, others gave themselves the challenge of other techniques such as acrostics and rhyming couplets.

Each piece in this collection shows the writers' dedication and imagination – we truly believe that seeing their work in print gives them a well-deserved boost of pride, and inspires them to keep writing, so we hope to see more of their work in the future!

CONTENTS

THE POEMS

In My Dreams

I see an adorable, furry fox
In a blue-spotted box
Wearing fluffy white socks
I see a cute cat
Sitting on a stripy mat
Wearing a colourful cotton-candy hat
He lives in a red flat
In my dreams
I see a blue bat
Sitting on my lap
I'm probably a scaredy-cat
In my dreams
I see me chasing
A bee
I am just a bear
Who doesn't care
I see a dog
In a bog
And now he's sitting on a log
How much weirder can this get?

Roni-Leigh Haines Ahmed (10)
Broom Barns Primary School, Stevenage

Rules Of The Jungle

There are four rules about the jungle,
Rule number one,
Make sure you don't mumble,
There are creatures lurking in the dark,
I hope someone's dog doesn't bark.
Rule number two,
Don't annoy the tiger,
Because he might bite ya.
Rule number three,
If you see a snake, make sure
You don't trip in the lake.
Rule number four,
Don't swing on the vines,
Because you might hurt your spine.

Teddy Overall (9)
Broom Barns Primary School, Stevenage

In My Dreams

In my dreams
I see a teacher
She loves technology
Her hobbies are making computer features

In my dreams
I see a dancer
She comes with her cat
Its name is Lancer

In my dreams
I see a wizard
He magically appears
With a lizard

In my dreams
I see a family
One is a teacher, the other one is a dancer
And the last one is a wizard.

Ivy Shonith (9)
Broom Barns Primary School, Stevenage

Once Upon A Dream

Once upon a dream
Just you and me
Living life peacefully
We both see a puppy
It's eating a gummy
Oh my god!
There is a bunny
She is really funny
Next we go flying over the cotton candy clouds
We reach my marshmallow house
With a chocolate roof
Then we go outside
To make a bond with the sun
It gives a warm smile back.

Rumaysa Latif (9)
Broom Barns Primary School, Stevenage

In The Winter Of My Dreams

In the winter, you can make a snowman.
In the winter, you can have a snowball fight.
In the winter, you can make snow angels.
In the winter, you can imagine that you have a Christmas tree.
In the winter, you can imagine decorating the Christmas tree.
In the winter, you can get presents underneath the Christmas tree.
Oh no, it's just a dream.

Zuzanna Misiewicz (9)
Broom Barns Primary School, Stevenage

Craziness Mayhem

In people's dreams
There are no beams.
There's a cute, fluffy fox
Sitting in a blue, stuffy box.
There is a pig called Peppa
Eating a big, spicy pepper.
There's a big, bad Barry
Holding my dad, Garry.
Now, I'm not happy,
I would rather wear a nappy.
How much worse can this get...

Hadeed Hassan (9)
Broom Barns Primary School, Stevenage

Warriors

Birds would sing loud and clear,
I would wake up like a bolt,
The air smelt very grotesque,
Brindlepaw was my new name,
Cats were surrounding me,
I knew this place! It was my book,
Someone offered me a rainbow trout,
They took me to a den just to realise,
I was not there...

Eva-Lily Connor (10)
Broom Barns Primary School, Stevenage

Mythical

I'm being chased by a centaur with potions.
I can't think about my emotions.
In the sky, there is a bird,
I think it was the third
Monster that I saw.
Maybe I was destined to be marked.
I looked into their eyes,
Deep inside, a lonely monster resides.

Robert Mantkines (9)
Broom Barns Primary School, Stevenage

The Infinite Ikea

So, I went to Ikea
To buy a new couch.
Then I realised I was trapped.
I was lazy so I slouched.
I had to stay safe,
So I had to build a base.
"Why?" you might be wondering, well you should know.
From the employees, of course, swinging a giant mace!

Nathan Kruslinski (9)
Broom Barns Primary School, Stevenage

Dreams Of Your Own

D reams come in all shapes and sizes
R ound and smooth
E ven if it's boring and small
A ll of them are different from each other
M ight as well say that it is perfect in your way
S o what do you think about your dream?

Vaanya Bhalothia (10)
Broom Barns Primary School, Stevenage

My Pets

I took good care of my dog Bear
Losing him would be a nightmare
Sometimes I let him sit in my new chair
My friends gave me a dare
To scare my dog Bear
I have a pet slime
But this is just a nursery rhyme
My mum tells me this is a waste of time.

Luca Best (10)
Broom Barns Primary School, Stevenage

Something Yummy

F antastic, my pizza is done, my favourite thing is
eating food.
O h, I just adore eating food, in fact, my hobby is
eating food.
O kay, you got me, but the only thing better than
eating food is
D oing things with my family.

Jacob Lo (10)
Broom Barns Primary School, Stevenage

I Went To McDonald's

In my dream
I live in a candy cane house
In my house, there is a mouse
He is my one and only pet
I cannot tell you how we first met

In my dream
I went to McDonald's
I saw a guy that was lean
His name was Ronald.

Daley Charlton (9)
Broom Barns Primary School, Stevenage

In People's Dreams

In people's dreams,
They see a fluffy fox,
Named Peppa.
They see a bear,
Named Gummy Bear.
Their cat is sad,
Just like their dad.
They see their puppy,
Eating a gummy.
They see their bear,
Taking care.

Ashkan Gorgani (10)
Broom Barns Primary School, Stevenage

Sweets

In my dream,
I see cotton candy
As fluffy as a cloud.
I see chocolate as
Hard as a rock.
I see toffee as
Sticky as a sweet.
I see Sour Patch Kids,
As sour as an apple.
I see a Fruit-tella,
As chewy as gum.

Lillia Dodds (10)
Broom Barns Primary School, Stevenage

In My Dreams

In my dreams,
There are loads of themes,
Any type,
There are loads of fruits that are ripe.
There is a person called Barry,
Who always tries to eat my dad Gary
There are video games,
There are also a lot of planes.

Zehraan Azam (9)
Broom Barns Primary School, Stevenage

My Dream

In my dream I see a small cute fox,
Lying on the box,
There is a ball,
Ryan kicks in the goal,
I'm riding my new bike,
and I am flying my kite,
I cut my chicken nuggets,
From KFC buckets.

Ryan Best (10)
Broom Barns Primary School, Stevenage

In The Land Of Dreams

In my dreams I imagine
A colourful rainbow gazing at me.
I imagine an exotic unicorn
Wearing a pink skirt, singing for me.
I imagine a hairy lion
Doing the cha cha cha, dancing for me.

Lexis Dundon (9)
Broom Barns Primary School, Stevenage

Poor Shrek

There once was a tall, silly man called poor Shrek,
He was so famous he met Ant and Dec,
His best friend was a donkey,
His face was all wonky,
That tall, silly man called poor Shrek.

Richie Thompkins (10)
Broom Barns Primary School, Stevenage

Sweet House

In my dream, I am a footballer.
I have a mansion filled
With Sour Patch Kids.
A whole room
Filled with chocolate.
Also a chocolate fountain
Filled with ice cream.

Jensen Smith (10)
Broom Barns Primary School, Stevenage

In My Dreams

There is a scaly dragon named Draco,
He lives in a cave called Paco,
He eats fish fingers coated with cocoa,
He plays football every day,
Having fun with his friend.

Harvey Norris (9)
Broom Barns Primary School, Stevenage

In My Dreams

In my dreams, I see a frog,
Sitting on a log,
I can see a bear,
Sitting on a chair,
In a home care.
I saw Mark,
His dog barked,
The tree had a bee.

Alfie Green (9)
Broom Barns Primary School, Stevenage

A Fox In My Dreams

In my dreams,
There's a fox
Wearing a green hat
And some grey socks
In a castle,
Riding a rainbow
Eating biscuits
All happening on the sun.

Nicholas Petri (10)
Broom Barns Primary School, Stevenage

Lion Vs Hyena

One night I went to bed and started dreaming...
I was a lion searching for my prey,
I saw the most weakest hyena ever seen,
I thought, *this will be easy because I am the strongest in the field anyway,*
The hyena was as ugly as a cracked open, rotten egg,
The hyena cackled as loud as can be,
I thought, *not a challenge,*
We fought, I won, obviously,
Dinner was served, my face was blood-covered,
I woke up and I was a lion wandering around.

Annie Porter (9)
Burghead Primary School, Burghead

Nightmares And Exciting Dreams

On tropical islands with people in camouflage
On streets with enormous titans
Sports cars crossing a bridge
Games taking over the world
Lost in a haunted mansion
Hearing strange voices
You're the greatest footballer
Everyone cheering for your team
Learning how to ride a bike
A van driving to Mars.

Findlay Maclean (9)
Burghead Primary School, Burghead

My Fantastic Football Dream

Running with the ball, past all the defenders
Whistling forward for the overhead kick
My heart racing as I take an amazing shot
Standing up to hold the World Cup
Skill after skill, I do as I play
Mountains of goals getting higher every day
Defenders trying to keep me at bay
Waking up on a midsummer's day.

Alex Turnbull (8)
Burghead Primary School, Burghead

My Football Dream

Running on a summer's day with a football at my feet.
Defenders trying to tackle.
I take a shot.
I thought I was going to miss but I don't.
I am working my socks off to get the Ballon d'Or.
Scores are 3-1 to us.
And then the Ballon d'Or winner is Owen Cameron.
I can't believe I won!

Owen Cameron (8)
Burghead Primary School, Burghead

I Had A Dream

I go to bed and I see...
A tropical island with lush trees and delicious coconuts.
Staggered rocks and poisonous spiders.
Erupting volcanoes all spewing out lava.
Ferocious birds swooping down to get their prey.
Cute monkeys jumping around in the trees.
Slimy snakes hiding in the grass.

Elliot Cakoni (9)
Burghead Primary School, Burghead

Dreams

It can be relaxing on the beach,
Drinking water and eating sweets,
In the hot sun,
Or up in the mountains,
With wind running down your feet,
Maybe you're in the desert with no food or water,
Or getting chased by a crazy-looking hen.

Reece Macinnes (9)
Burghead Primary School, Burghead

Nightmare

Creepy monsters around,
Coming closer by the second,
Ominous noises start to appear,
While my heart is racing,
It's so dark, I cannot see a glimpse of light,
I don't see a single way out,
Until morning when I wake up again.

Daisy Murrie (9)
Burghead Primary School, Burghead

Mechanical

Call every minute of the day.
Crashing cars everywhere I go.
Parts slowly running out.
Repairing cars left, right and centre.
Prices going up like a rocket.
Engines like a tornado.
Brakes as stiff as a steering wheel.

Connor Harrison (7)
Burghead Primary School, Burghead

Tropical

Nice beaches,
Warm water,
Sandcastles everywhere,
Boats flying,
Fish swimming,
Drinks as sweet as candyfloss.
Villas everywhere,
Palm trees,
Sun shining,
Exquisite food,
Sunbeds soft like snow.

Muir MacDougall (9)
Burghead Primary School, Burghead

Gymnastic Competition

Standing in a stadium.
Everyone cheering.
Friends watching everyone.
People winning medals.
Children crying with happiness.
Gymnasts cheering for their friends.
People waving flags.
Judges giving scores.

Mhairi Swadel (8)
Burghead Primary School, Burghead

Spy Adventure

Spy I wish to be.
Cool gadgets
Spy suit generator.
Spy training
Gonna be the best spy ever.
High score, taking over the world.
Highjacked off a boat or plane
To the King of High Score's Lair.

Isla Henry (8)
Burghead Primary School, Burghead

My Strange Dream

I go to sleep and what I see is,
Sheep flying through the air,
Planes flying people,
Birds waddling in fields,
Trees jumping down the street,
Selling cows at Tesco.
Why so strange?

Harry Orme (9)
Burghead Primary School, Burghead

Devil

The thought of a devil.
A devil is dark.
As dark as dawn.
Deep in a cave.
Bats dashing down the cave.
Devil's dashing at the bats.
Bats dashing to get away.

Arran Ramsay (9)
Burghead Primary School, Burghead

Tropical Beach

Dream as cool as a leopard,
Thick orange branches on a tropical beach,
Leopards chasing me in the pitch-black,
Clothes getting ripped,
Wooden axes flying through the air.

Ross Watson (8)
Burghead Primary School, Burghead

Medieval Mayhem

"It's 3am in the morning, Mum," groaned Daniel.
"Don't care, get up you bum!" shouted Mum.
"Where are we? Am I dreaming?" asked Daniel.
"No, you're eating!" exclaimed Mum.
"Why's King Arthur outside?" asked Daniel.
"Don't know, think he needs a ride," suggested Mum.
"Hey look, it's Robin Hood," revealed Daniel.
"Don't disturb him, he's in a bad mood," nagged Jona.
"Oh, there's a wee white rabbit," whispered Daniel.
"Hey! Don't grab it," mumbled Jona.
"And that's what I did in my dream," proclaimed Daniel.
"So now I'm going to go for a swim in the river stream," stated Daniel.

Daniel Pringle (11)
Cleeves Primary School, Glasgow

My Special Class

When I was young,
I wanted to be an astronaut.
Then I thought, *why not?!*
Then I woke up, I wasn't flying.
I looked up and almost started crying.
Then Jim said he was dying.
The teacher said, "Jim, you're lying."
Then Ben blabbered, he was a bird!
Oops, that's the wrong word.
After that, my teacher said,
"She doesn't get paid enough!"
With a big puff!
"Samantha, why are you eating a mouse?"
"Jim, you're not a house!"
Then the bell rang.
I gasped, "Thank god!"

Riley Russell (11)
Cleeves Primary School, Glasgow

The Valley

N o, no! Uh, this place again?
I should not be here for the fifth time.
G lancing about as I start to climb.
H uh, that smell is disgusting
T his place reeks of death, there's a chill in the air.
M y... what is that? Uh, I'm going away.
A demon is what it is, it's name is Soak. I better hide.
R eally? Oh, come on. This has to be a joke!
E h? It was all a nightmare! I realised as I woke.

Daniel Tennant (11)
Cleeves Primary School, Glasgow

Monsters

M y heart dropped as it hopped under my bed.
O nly if this was not real.
N ow I think this is the real deal.
S hadows all over my room.
"T ime to hide," it said, I'm shocked.
E ven though it was too late, I snuggled up in my duvet.
R elieved as I thought it was gone.
S omething popped up ahead.

But it was all in my head.

Layla Harrison (11)
Cleeves Primary School, Glasgow

Demonic

D reaming of terrifying bloody rooms.
E verything screaming in agony and terror.
M enacing giants beaming down at me while I walk.
O ver the seas of dead bodies and skeletons.
N ightmare that nobody could ever forget.
I wake up with relief, I thought I was dead.
C rying, my mother burst into my room and I went back to sleep.

David Colquhoun (11)
Cleeves Primary School, Glasgow

A Class Teacher's Nightmare

Why is this class such a riot?
Bob, just be quiet!
James, stop throwing your toys!
Samantha, stop kissing the boys!
Mason, why are you crying?
No, Arron, you're not dying!
No, Harry, you don't have a hundred homes!
Jake, stop trying to break your bones!
Why is this class like a daycare?
Argh! Thank god it's just a nightmare.

Max Lloyd (11)
Cleeves Primary School, Glasgow

The Chasing Clown

C ackling and laughing coming from the hallway,
L onely in my room, I'm terrified,
O nly if this was a dream! No! It's chasing me!
W hen I was running I tripped,
N ow I'm up and I crawled into bed,
S afely I lay in my bed, suddenly I woke up, it was all in my head!

Charlotte Stewart (11)
Cleeves Primary School, Glasgow

Pirates And Ships

Pirates riot in the ship,
Pirates fighting everywhere.
Cannonballs flying everywhere,
Our ship was sinking.
We were thinking what to do,
But the marine was here.
We asked for help but they never helped,
But it was all a dream.

Rahool Habibzai (11)
Cleeves Primary School, Glasgow

Day Of A Football Player

I am a famous football player.
My luxury house has a diamond-blue swimming pool.
My stairs are made of fluff.
The ceiling is made of carrot cake
And blueberry muffins
Mouldy cheese and Irn Bru.
Someone just broke into my house!

Gary Cullen (11)
Cleeves Primary School, Glasgow

Clowns

C lowns are as scary as a snake,
L aughing so hard, they made me more scared,
O h they made me nervous,
W ith huge grins,
N ever, they smile.
S omehow I always see them.

Mubeen Fatima (11)
Cleeves Primary School, Glasgow

Untitled

C lowns are scary.
L ong shoes.
O range, red, green, blue, all of them.
W ith huge faces.
N ot real smiles.
S omehow always hideous.

Thomas Cargill (11)
Cleeves Primary School, Glasgow

Space Lily

S pace is a big part of Lily the penguin!
P lanets that Lily lives on, Pluto is where it's cold. Pluto is where her friends live. She has good friends to play with.
A stronauts want to take me away to see if I'm a new alien
C apturing aliens is her favourite hobby
E arth is so small when I look at it from my home.

L ily's friend is Alex and Alex is her friend
I t is so nice to see space but the mean monkeys are annoying
L ittle aliens come to my home and try and put my purple light in when I am not home
Y esterday she went to school. "We are both happy!" said Lily and Alex.

Diana Jukse (10)
Gilford Primary School, Gilford

Going To Space Dream

Large rockets zooming through space!
It makes me so excited, I want to race.
They fly so fast.
I wish it would always last!

They go up and down and all around.
If you're on the moon, there's no sound.
It's so fun!
It's like eating a chocolate bun!

In space, you might think there's not much.
But if you go, there's so much stuff, you couldn't put it in one bag.
But when you wake up, don't feel sad,
Because there's always tonight, so don't feel bad.

Finlay Fitzpatrick (10)
Gilford Primary School, Gilford

Gilford Primary

G oing on amazing trips.
I Pad games.
L ovely classes.
F ood from the dinner hall.
O n the green screen.
R acing on sports day.
D oing PE.

P laying with friends outside.
R emembering to bring your homework.
I also love reading books from the library.
M athletics tasks to do.
A nd bring in a pencil case.
R emember to be kind.
Y ou need to know all your times tables.

Eva Grant (8)
Gilford Primary School, Gilford

A Shetland Pony Called Ginger

There once was a shetland pony called Ginger
Who wished she was a horse
But she didn't have the force.
She was silly
Like her friend, Billy.
She would dance and prance like a deer
But she didn't have the cheer.
She went to the field
And Billy revealed
He had been attacked by a bear
With really long hair.
He said he was fine
But I think he was just thinking about time.
I saw a puddle
That was in a muddle.
My walking was so subtle.

Emily Heak (9)
Gilford Primary School, Gilford

Faithful Fireworks

They rise like sudden, fiery flowers that burst upon the night
Then fall to the earth in burning showers of crimson, blue and white
Like flowers too wonderful to name

Each miracle unfolds, and Ferris wheels begin to flame like whirling marigolds
Rockets and Roman candles make an orchard of the sky

Whence majestic trees shake their elegant petals upon each glaring eye
They express the most extravagant 'hey'
Our immaculate firework display.

Grace Cobley (10)
Gilford Primary School, Gilford

Sparks In The Sky

Standing in the middle of the gorgeous park,
Looking up in the dark,
As I heard a big *bang!*
And my ears rang,

There were vibrant fireworks in the sky,
But it was up very high,
They rose like fiery flowers blooming,
While they were quickly zooming.

As they faded away in the distance, far away,
Bang! Is the only thing they say,
When I woke up, I had a spark,
But all alone in the dark.

Bella McCaulsky (10)
Gilford Primary School, Gilford

Roller Coaster Nightmare

Once upon a dream...

I went on something very fast,
It was quite vast,
I barely reached the height requirement,
Luckily, I was in the right environment.

The roller coaster was so scary,
I was not very merry,
I shouted so loud,
I was the loudest of the crowd.

It was in a new park,
We rode it in the dark,
The roller coaster broke like cream,
And then, I realised it was all a dream.

Isaac Overend (9)
Gilford Primary School, Gilford

A Nightmare

It was a blistering day,
So I started to make clay,
Of course the day broke,
Next, I had a can of Coke.

But it started to get quite cloudy,
The house began to get really shouty,
The sky became dark,
Next, the dog began to bark.

Then appeared a dreadful monster,
He said his name was Prowler,
His chest shot a mighty beam,
Finally I realised it was all a dream.

Alex Bolton (10)
Gilford Primary School, Gilford

The Bear

I was in a forest with a bear
He was combing his hair
He loved flowers.
He made fun of his friends with enjoyment

He had a family
They were a decent family who would never be dishonest
The bear, I helped him tie his tie

He pulled on his Crocs and acted like a fox
I ran into a creepy house
And got a mop and hit a cop
And I got arrested by a cop.

Amelija Pranyte (9)
Gilford Primary School, Gilford

Football Dream

There was a blinding flash of white light,
A curtain appeared and I pulled it away, out of my sight.
Then a light as bright as day,
Took me away from the realities of today.

My alarm woke me up,
Then my mum's shrill voice made me jump,
"What a dream," I muttered to myself,
As I took my homework from my shelf.

Lois Maramba Brabetz (10)
Gilford Primary School, Gilford

Fabulous Fireworks

Fabulous fireworks swirl across the sky,
Oh, how they soar up so high,
The beautiful colours explode in the air,
The fireworks let off a gorgeous flare.

The sky is filled with vibrant colours,
And so many others,
I can't take my eyes away from them,
The sky is sparkling like a gem.

Annie Martin (10)
Gilford Primary School, Gilford

Running Away From The Zombies

Terrifying in the abandoned house.
When I see a zombie mouse.
If I scream.
Then the zombie's eyes will gleam.

I am up so high.
I might cry.
I am so scared.
From below, the zombie's eyes stare.

I suddenly wake up in my sweat-filled bed.
I dashingly wipe my head.

Grace Mccann (9)
Gilford Primary School, Gilford

Flaming Fire

I had a dream.
Where the kitchen filled up with steam.
There was a wire.
That must have caught on fire.
I wanted to scream.

I saw my cat.
Hiding in a hat.
Then I ran for my life.
But I figured out it was just a dream.
There was really no need to scream.

Sally Martin (8)
Gilford Primary School, Gilford

Billy And His Friend

A little girl called Andy loved candy.
She was handy.
She was pretty like her friend Billy.
Billy was so silly.
Billy loved hats.
He had a pet rat.
He sat on a hat.
He wanted a pet bat.
Billy never did a crime.
He loved to rhyme.
He was always on time.

Isabella Duprey (9)
Gilford Primary School, Gilford

Being Chased By A Lot Of Big Spiders

Being chased by a lot of big spiders
And a lot of riders
And then they all came through the door
And then they all came to get a lot more
They all were here and their legs were tight
And they got into a fight
And there was a beam
And there was a lot of cream.

Adam Nicholl (8)
Gilford Primary School, Gilford

The Horse Called Porsh

I've got a new horse that is called Porsh.
He always has force.
He loves to trot.
But his foot always rots.
When he trots on locks.
He thinks they are rocks.

He wears a hat.
And acts like a bat.
He likes cats.
And lies down on the mat.

Ariya Byrne (9)
Gilford Primary School, Gilford

Going To The Moon

I am on the moon
It is very cold and old
It is like I am flying
I have no food at all.
I have been sitting on
A rock all day.
It is so cold.
It is May.
I am trying to
Find some water.

Alfie Ferguson (8)
Gilford Primary School, Gilford

Plane Dream

I was on a plane with a friend called Zane
We were in the sky, we thought we could fly
I started to sing a song, Zane sang along
I said, "I can't wait to land," and then saw sand.

Kayden Dale (8)
Gilford Primary School, Gilford

My Morning

I get up out of bed
Get washed and fed
Then it's off to school
I must be there for nine
As that's the rule.

Jamie-Lee Toal (9)
Gilford Primary School, Gilford

Clowns

C reepy clowns in the woods, all I can wonder is if I try to run they might catch me,
L urking in the dark, the clowns are looking for me and my dog,
O n my way to run to a dog walker to ask for help, to beg them to call someone,
W ithout warning, the clowns jump out and chase me and my dog, but not the lady, I cry in a heap but I just can't any more,
N ow they have caught me and taped my mouth with duct tape,
S cared, I kept whining, "Help," and that moment they took the tape off and revealed they were my friends, as we walked home I was still terrified.

Darci Maxam (9)
Goddard Park Primary School, Park North

When I Grow Up I Will Be A Footballer

Part 1
When I grow up, I wish I could be a footballer
Because I play football and football is my thing
So I want to be a footballer when I grow up
My T-shirt will say Hamley 24
And I will play for Swindon
I hopefully should win
But sometimes I would lose.

Part 2
F or exercise
O ur friend forever
O nly for some people
T he best game ever
B e kind to everyone in a match
A lways smile
L isten to everyone
L isten to the referee.

Lola Hamley (9)
Goddard Park Primary School, Park North

Dancer Dragons

Once there lived a dragon,
She had a dream to be a dancer.
She practised every day and night.

It made her tired,
But she didn't give up.
Finally, the day came,
To share her knowledge.

She did some line dancing,
Street dance and ballet.
Everyone was stumped,
Then a huge applause came!

She taught the big and the small,
Soon everyone was dancing.

Ruby Zakarauskite (9)
Goddard Park Primary School, Park North

Lost In York

My friends and me ran away from our school trip
But then we got lost!
There were two thieves there called Harry and Marv
That were haunting us
So we decided to prank them
And then we went outside but they caught us
Then Harry took out his gun
And then Arayn showed up
He got a lot of bird seeds and threw it at them
Then they got arrested.

Omari Bramble (9)
Goddard Park Primary School, Park North

The Land Of The Clowns

In a land of laughs and kooky sighs,
A group of clowns led wild delights.
Their noses red, their shoes absurd,
They brought joy with every word.

They turned and stumbled, oh what a sight.
Tripping over their oversized shoes with all their might.
Their pants were baggy, their hats were tall,
They made everyone giggle, both big and small.

With faces painted in colours so bright,
They chased away sadness with all their might.

But there was one clown, the king of fun,
Who had a mishap, every time he spun.
He'd juggle balls, but they'd soar so high,
And land on someone's head with a loud, "Why?"

They decided that was the end of the amazing show.

Abdelrahman Nouri (10)
Hallfield Primary School, Westminster

Stuck In A Paradise!

Lost in a paradise, a dream come true,
But trapped in its beauty, with no way through,
The sun shines bright, the ocean so blue,
I'm surrounded with trees, oh look, a kangaroo!

I need to get out, I have to find a way,
Despite its treasures, "I have to leave," I say!
The birds sing sweetly, the flowers bloom,
But I'm stuck in this paradise longing to resume.

The sand between my toes, my legs start to hurt,
I've been walking aimlessly with dirt in my shirt!
With waves that crash and seagulls' call,
I'll cherish this paradise big and small.

Ava Ahaidyar (10)
Hallfield Primary School, Westminster

Ghost Orchid

G hosts have come to haunt the town!
H idden away from blizzard lights,
O minously opening their pale buds (Ghost Orchid, Queen of Flowers)
S winging with the handsome breeze,
T ilting their heads and polite and serene, (Ghost Orchid, Queen of Flowers)

O scillating to and from their perches,
R eeling in victims of their dance,
C autious and you'll be safe from those
H aunting masked queens.
I f you don't then despair, you'll fall under the spell of
D endrophylax lindenii, Queen of the Ghost.

Huda Ali (9)
Hallfield Primary School, Westminster

Galactic Dreams

Among the stars, a comic melody,
Planets and moons in perfect harmony.
With swirling colours and celestial sights,
The universe dazzles with its infinite lights.

Galaxies collide, creating a cosmic show,
In this, vast wonders continue to grow.
Stars twinkle in the night, shining so bright,
Constellation swirling, a mesmerising sight.

The Milky Way, our cosmic home,
A tapestry of stars where we roam.
Each planet is unique with its own special place,
The hugeness of space, it leaves us amazed.

Mason Bustarde (9)
Hallfield Primary School, Westminster

Football

When I score a goal, the fans go mad,
Oh no! We're scoring 3-1 and now I'm really sad,
I don't know why this defender is so tall,
But look! I nutmegged him and made him fall.

Oh! I scored!
I'm actually not that bored.
I hate the goalkeeper, Patrick,
Because he's stopping me from getting my hat-trick.

Ah! I tackle the midfielder,
It's me against Alexander,
I go around him and I score.
Six months later, I win the Ballon d'Or.

Areeb Asif (10)
Hallfield Primary School, Westminster

The Dragon And The Gem

I go to bed every night and travel back in time through the light.
I wake in a cave that's cold to see lots of gold.
I light a flame, wow! All this treasure will bring me fame.
As I walk deeper into this wondrous cave, I start to feel nervous.
My eye catches a sparkle, gosh, that green gem is high up.
Uh oh, I hear a crackle nearby!
The scaly dragon stomps towards me and
Chomps its terrible teeth.
The dragon's tail swooped and its fire looped.
I run and I run.
And now after I go to bed every night,
I always wake in a terrible fright.

Max Gudger (8)
Higham-On-The-Hill Church Of England Primary School, Nuneaton

Springtime

Past the winter, before the summer that is the season of spring,
Sun, flowers, happy days and new beginnings it brings.

Baby animals in the fields,
Dancing and jumping with excited squeals.

Hopping and jumping with newborn glee,
Frolicking and feeding and chasing a bee.

Cheerful chicks chirping in their coops,
On their tiny stick legs waddling in troupes.

Daffodils and daisies in the meadows,
Lavender and rosemary in the hedgerows.

Leila-Rose Doherty (11)
Higham-On-The-Hill Church Of England Primary School, Nuneaton

Lost In Town

I went to town,
But now I frown!
I'm lost with my brother,
We look for my mother.
I don't know what to do,
But I stop to wonder whether this is true.
Maybe take the bus or maybe take the train,
I don't know but I am in a lot of pain.
I don't know what to do or say,
No matter what I'm stuck inside my brain.
As I walk around I keep my frown,
Until I see what looks like a mystery.
Instead me and my brother see our mother!

Alexis Munene (10)
Higham-On-The-Hill Church Of England Primary School, Nuneaton

Unicorn Dreams

U nicorns living angelically, tired ones, happy ones
N othing could break their special bonds
I magine them falling apart like it could ever happen
C onfused, I heard the sound of a gunshot, it was like a cannon
O r it was a bomb going off
R eally running like a cheetah made us huff and puff
N ow everything is settled and we're all cosy in the house.

Moyo Akinkoye (9)
Higham-On-The-Hill Church Of England Primary School, Nuneaton

Winter Robin

Hey little robin
Sitting on my
Window
What are you doing in the
Ice-cold snow?
Being
All orange and
Red
Would you like to
Sit on my
Bed?
Come in little robin
And take a nice
Warm glow
Before you go
Back out
In the
Snow.

Lennon Crawley (10)
Higham-On-The-Hill Church Of England Primary School, Nuneaton

The Hockey Final

As I step onto the pitch, I look around
I get nervous and dizzy, my head starts to pound
I look at the Belgian boys,
And all the crowd making lots of noise
As I start to remember all my hard work
My hands start to jerk,
As the referee blows his whistle
Wishing I had some rain, just a drizzle
I get the ball
Send an aerial to Paul
He takes it with ease
And does a squeeze
Over their stick
Their defender crumbles like a brick
Crossed it into the D
Just like our coach, Paddy
We get it in the shooting zone
Whoosh! Bang!
It hits the backboard
We might have set an Irish record
Ireland were the victors
But we all had blisters,

I look up at the crowd,
And feel very proud,
To play for my nation,
And we throw a big celebration.

Conor Brown (11)
Inchmarlo Preparatory School, Belfast

The Ship

I found myself on a deserted island,
I was very confused.
I saw palm trees as tall as giraffes,
And a gigantic, abandoned ship.
I went to explore,
The ship was creaking in the wind.
I climbed up and entered through a crack.
I was in, but an avalanche of debris blocked the door,
And looming in the darkness, was a skeleton!
It came alive,
And it had a sword.
The fight ensued.
Clash! Clink! went the swords,
But then it stabbed me!
I thought I was dead,
But then I woke up!

Caleb Milligan (11)
Inchmarlo Preparatory School, Belfast

Once Upon A Dream

You're somewhere,
You're in a cave,
Hope you're brave!
In the dark, gosh it is dark,
Nothing like a park!
Quiet and freezing cold,
A glorious cave, empty of gold,
In the inky soup,
You fumble on the ground,
You turn around,
A spooky, scary clown!
You dash ahead,
Into the dark,
You spot light!
It's following you,
You enter the light,
You're in a bloodstained room,
The room is white,
Lit by lights,
And wake in bed!

Sebastian Parsons (11)
Inchmarlo Preparatory School, Belfast

In The Clouds

I go to my bed at night
To enter my dream for tonight
As I enter my dream,
I am met with a surprise

I am in the clouds
High up in the sky
Looking down,
I see I can fly

I am flying in the clouds very, very high
A plane flies by,
Birds next to me
It's so wonderful to fly.

But then I awake from my wonderful dream
Only to hear outside my bedroom door
"Wake up, it's 8:12,
We are going to be late to school again!"

Ethan Whalley (11)
Inchmarlo Preparatory School, Belfast

The Dream Derby

Cheers, shouting, screaming, then I look up,
And I see a scoreboard 2-2 Man United - Man City, 89th minute,
Then I start to focus,
I see Haaland going through on goal,
Doing a hocus pocus,
He spins past the keeper,
Everybody is in shock; I'm the last player,
He shoots,
I run as fast as I can,
Then I jump in the way, I header it off the line,
But break my spine by hitting it off the post,
And I wake up,
To the smell of my mum making toast.

Teddy Hamil (11)
Inchmarlo Preparatory School, Belfast

Paintings On The Wall

I wake up in a dark room,
With pictures on the wall
Of a sad groom,
Then I feel a sudden call,
Why is she crying on the wall?
Curious me, I keep walking up
The dark narrow hall.
Walk, run, hop and jump,
With paintings, big small, little and tall.

And finally, it ends,
I wake up cosy in my bed,
I go to school and tell my friends,
What was going on up there,
In my head.

Sebastian Simpson (11)
Inchmarlo Preparatory School, Belfast

The Forest

In my dreams every night
I wake up in a
Big, dark, scary forest.
The trees blow recklessly
In the wind.
The wolf's howl is louder
Than a siren.

The owls hunt all night long.
A scary clown hunts you
Down all through the dream
And of course, there is a
Big, dark, scary house
In the middle of the forest.
And finally, you wake up
In your nice comfy
Bed.

Daniel McCarter (11)
Inchmarlo Preparatory School, Belfast

I Close My Eyes

I close my eyes
And I drift away,
I enter strange worlds
And night turns to day,
Trees that talk
And clowns that chase,
Floors like lava
And winning the race,
Spiders in my bed
And flying through the sky,
Looking for my brother
And thinking he might die,
Bouncing in bubbles
And hearing people scream,
Anything could happen
When I close my eyes to dream.

Felix Harrison (10)
Inchmarlo Preparatory School, Belfast

Treasure And Me

T reasure is what I dig for
R aking in money every single day
E very day I am happier
A nd every single day me and my dragon are happier
S cared looks far below as me and my dragon are fierce
U sing my money on a lovely house for me and my dragon
R eaching further every day
E very second, me and my dragon are happier

A nd every second me and my dragon are happier
N ever will I hate my dragon
D arting around, finding treasure

M e and my dragon fly
E very second me and my dragon are happier.

Reece Mauro (9)
Little Heath Primary School, Potters Bar

The Dream That Went Wrong

I lie in my snug bed,
And close my weary eyes,
What will I dream of today,
It's always a nice surprise,

When suddenly I'm in a forest,
With snow-topped, stately trees,
It's oh so frosty,
With a bitter cold breeze,

Petrified, curious,
That is how I feel,
But it's impossible to stay alive
This can't be real!

I stumble across an intimidating ice wall
But stare up at the stars,
They are shining so bright,
That aeons can not vex or tire,

Stuck in my little daydream,
I fall down a never-ending hole,
I try to grab something,
Maybe a stick or a pole!

A portal opens before me,
A glimmering circle of light,
Inviting and beckoning me,
A circle that is so bright

Suddenly, I am back in bed,
Millions of thoughts swim in my head,
I look up at my clothes, and there is proof!
Snow-coated clothes, like a second blanket and no snow on the roof!

I guess this wasn't a dream after all,
I think I'll always remember it,
I don't think it is possible,
Not even a little bit.

Shraddha Iyengar
Little Heath Primary School, Potters Bar

Horror Lands

H orror Lands are a place of mischievous events happening every day,
O ver hills and mountains lie dangerous things,
R evolting clowns jumping out from a cave,
R oaring bats the size of cats fly above my head,
O ut of nowhere appear screeching birds as loud as sirens,
R eaching hands are after you, so watch out,

L urking in the caves are horrific monsters,
A horrible creature's lair is in the abyss,
N o one leaves until they wake up,
D arkness is petrifying for all creatures,
S piders hang from creepy branches.

Serenity Slaytor (9)
Little Heath Primary School, Potters Bar

Mystic Mandy

I wake up to go downstairs in the night,
I'm scared I might get a fright,
The worst thing is, it's night, so where's my kite?

I'm in the living room,
Suddenly I hear a boom!
It could have just been Mum,
Mum, that's not fun!

Is that a unicorn?
I might need to respawn!
This can't be real,
Hey! I've got a pet seal.

This has to be a joke.
Mum, if this is real, give me a Coke,
I'm Mandy,
I'm John.

You now turn into mystic Mandy,
Don't listen to the people at school.
No more Mandy Dandy.

Autumn Williams (9)
Little Heath Primary School, Potters Bar

The Dragon

I was riding on a dragon,
Its scales so bright,
Its mouth alight,
With a tail as sharp as a knife.

Its saddle was brown and worn down,
Riding over a town,
Its smile so wide,
As we flew over a tide.

It was 9 AD,
The village was cheerful and bright,
Birds chirping all through the night,
As we turned to the right,
We saw a spectacular sight.

As the ground grew closer,
A hurricane stormed inside my head,
We halted to a stop,
On a perch in my window,
He carried me to bed,
One... two... three,
I woke up, and he was gone.

Joseph Gandolfini (9)
Little Heath Primary School, Potters Bar

A Unicorn Dream

A t every corner

U nicorns dance,
N ever would I have thought that I would meet a unicorn,
I ntriguing colours of the world catch my eye.
C ombinations of purple and pink,
O h, this is amazing,
R avenous creatures wouldn't dare to step in,
N ever, ever would I want to leave.

D ancing in the wind,
R apids come rushing down,
E ntering places I didn't know existed.
A mazingly, my life has changed,
M agical flowers scent the air! Dreamland!

Rafaella-Maria Polydorou (9)
Little Heath Primary School, Potters Bar

The Clown Shed

One night I lay down in my bed,
And woke up in a shed,
I was shivering in the cold,
But I wanted to feel bold,
The place was covered in blood,
And outside was mud.

The place was ancient and dead,
Then I found myself awake in my bed,
The next night,
I woke up somewhere bright,
I rode my bike,
To somewhere I like.

Suddenly, I stumbled upon a spoke,
I accidentally fell over my bike,
Then I got a fright,
The clowns looked like they bite,
I ran for my life.

Chloe Hathaway (10)
Little Heath Primary School, Potters Bar

Nature Is Amazing

Nature is amazing,
With its gracing,
While the dancing blossoms float gently down,
The sun happily plays hide-and-seek with the clouds,
In fields overwhelmed with greenery.

Nature is amazing,
With its gracing,
While the sun shines like a star,
The colourful parrots chirp,
In the rainbow sparkling sky.

Nature is amazing,
With its gracing,
And the trees brushing the clouds,
The feeling of the gentle breeze surrounding me,
This is life.

Madhurya Ananthakrishnan (10)
Little Heath Primary School, Potters Bar

Bedtime Dream

B eautiful fairies dancing in the moonlight,
E xquisite flowers blooming,
D oubtful faces,
T reacherous mountains as high as the sky itself,
I magination running wild,
M agnificent views,
E xtraordinary dreams from you.

D octor Suess flying through the air,
R uthless giants storming through,
E lephants bounding along too,
A nimals everywhere,
M onstrous nightmares there to dread.

Winter Barrett (10)
Little Heath Primary School, Potters Bar

The Land Of Sweets

I woke up in a magical land,
But all I could see was loads of sand,
Cakes, lollipops and chocolate river,
I like this dream, it's not so bitter,
I soon found a round, fluffy creature,
It told me its name was Beater,
Beater and I travelled out far,
We soon realised there was a caramel bar,
We found a sword and shield,
Before darkness fell over the field,
I woke up and realised it was a dream,
Then I started to eat ice cream.

Leo Cooper (9)
Little Heath Primary School, Potters Bar

A Whole New World

This world isn't like any other
People flying but losing direction
I see that I'm all alone
A dragon with glazing breath comes to me
He throws me onto his scaly back
I am frightened and can't believe my eyes
I am safe
I am safe
The dragon places me down on the lumpy ground
Then I trip, but I don't know how
Then I am levitating on the ground
I say, "Wow!" but realise it was all a dream.

Chloe Sorodoc (10)
Little Heath Primary School, Potters Bar

The Ancient Dreams

I wake up and go downstairs.
A *whoosh* of cold air comes by.
Boom! I see my living room is Antarctica.
I see a penguin waddling across my path.

I magically get teleported to ancient Greek times,
On the ruby-red race track with that penguin.
Bang! The whistle goes and I sprint and turn.
I win and the crowd goes with whooos and cheers.
No! I woke up, what a bummer!

Lily Irwin (9)
Little Heath Primary School, Potters Bar

In The Darkness

As I wake up, I'm in the middle of nowhere,
I can see a massive fortress in front of me.
I start to panic, this can't be real, where's my family?
But then I black out and collapse to the floor.

After, I wake up in a dark room with no one with me,
I wait for hours and hours until,
I see a giant opening the door, arghh!
But then I wake up sweating and relieved that it's over.

Seb Sleet (10)
Little Heath Primary School, Potters Bar

Yes Or No?

Y es or no?
E levator or lift?
S cooby-Doo thinks elevator, but he's American.

O r is it you who's American?
R ight now, it doesn't matter, all that matters is...

N o, or yes.
O ctopuses think Scooby-Doo is wrong, and so do I! I wake up. Phew, I didn't do that homework! Wait, I didn't do that homework!

Bobby Speer-Morgan (9)
Little Heath Primary School, Potters Bar

The Land Of Espada

The land of Espada is a wonderful place,
For the immense space makes me want to run and race,
My steed, my serpent and my dragon are all mighty,
While I start to cry and hold my pets tightly.
I have my life very calmly
Looking at the pink sky and the lush green palm trees,
Suddenly I start to fade away,
And wake up in my bed at the start of another day.

Stirling McIntyre (9)
Little Heath Primary School, Potters Bar

A Magical Wonderland

A magical wonderland is what I see,
Am I stuck on this land, or is it a dream?
At least I have company to keep my guide,
If I go crazy, footballer Messi will come and help me,
Together we'll search for clues to get off this land,
Get all the clues and get out of here,
Time to go before the doors close,
Bye-bye now, it's time to go.

Prince Stewart (9)
Little Heath Primary School, Potters Bar

The Glare Of A Nightmare

My mum's glare is a nightmare,
Her eyes narrow with her nightmare glare,
Her stare is bad, but she's got a nightmare glare,
When I'm in bed, the haunt of her nightmare glare is there.

When she glares, I feel compared,
The room is dark when she glares,
Her glare is as ugly as her hair,
Her stare and glare are a pair.

Finlay McGregor (10)
Little Heath Primary School, Potters Bar

Pirate Panic

I wake up on a ship,
The hammock I'm on soon will rip,
I'm on the floor, dazed and confused,
Cannonballs are flying that are old and used,
A Kraken is there and is destroying the boat,
He pulls me down but I can't float,
Once I wake, I am gasping for air,
That was not a nice time,
That was a nightmare.

Jorgo Karavokyri (10)
Little Heath Primary School, Potters Bar

The Shadow

I am in the dark,
Following a spark,
There is no light to see,
So this might be,
A scary story for me,

Leaves dancing in the breeze,
I might just freeze,
Then the light appears,
And a shadow disappears,
I run a bit,
So I do not lose it,
Then I find all of them,
In their little den.

Raynell Obeng (10)
Little Heath Primary School, Potters Bar

Dream Life

Outside blue skies ahead,
Trees swaying, fresh green grass for miles,
Scorching hot sun, heating up your skin instantly,
Hair swaying many times,
Fields filled with fantastic animals that can enjoy the wildlife around them,
Loving every second on that hot summer's day,
Instantly you want to stay there forever.

Toby Phillips (10)
Little Heath Primary School, Potters Bar

Wonderland

I get out of my bed,
Seeing nothing but red,
The red disappears,
As I shout two cheers,
A soul appears
I wipe my eyes,
Greeted by five pies,
I stand up nice and tall,
Walking down a mysterious hall,
I get to the end,
Seeing a world blend,
I wake up,
Moaning about my luck.

Zack Gottesman (9)
Little Heath Primary School, Potters Bar

World Cup

World Cup, the air is dark
World Cup, the final is up
World Cup, I need to win the cup
World Cup, the other team scored
World Cup, *goal*, we're back
World Cup, our team is stuck
World Cup, it's penalties now
World Cup, *goal!*
We win the cup.

Oscar Lovell (9)
Little Heath Primary School, Potters Bar

Dreamland

D reamland with lots of sounds,
R ipe fruit all around,
E very day there's a smile,
A cross every mile,
M usicians beating,
L aughing and meeting,
A pples fall from tall trees,
N ever a breeze,
D reamland.

Emma Charvet-Quemin Dotor (9)
Little Heath Primary School, Potters Bar

The Dino Realm

I woke up in a field, dark and grey,
Pterodactyls swooped away,
All I wanted was to play,
But a caveman shouted, "Hey!"
I said, "Do you want to play?"
He punched me in the head, and said, "Hooray!"
The dream is over.

Chris Petrides (10)
Little Heath Primary School, Potters Bar

The Adventures Of Pandora

Volcanoes erupting everywhere,
There was lots of lava around me,
The air was full of toxic gas,
I just wanted to hide in a glass jar,
If I breathed that in, then I would die.

It was way too dangerous.

Jessica Anstey (9)
Little Heath Primary School, Potters Bar

Confused World

The world is always upside down,
So no one is walking on the ground.
I hope this isn't real,
Sort it out quicker than a turning of a wheel!

Amy Billing (10)
Little Heath Primary School, Potters Bar

Down In The Dark

Don't get out of bed, it might snatch your leg,
Don't get out crying, or it will creep up behind you like a slithering snake,
Don't stir, don't shake; it might have you for its next snack!
Don't look under your bed, or it will be game over for you,
It has shiny, vivid eyes that glisten in the sky,
It has knife-sharp talons, especially for you,
So that's why you don't look under your bed,
It's alright in the morning, or is it a dream?
Yes, it could be.
Only one way to make sure, back under your bed!

Luka Polloway (8)
Mary Exton Primary School, Hitchin

My Dream World

M y world is free from audism, sexism and racism.
Y ou won't get bullied, ever.

D on't you try to be rude,
R ude! Off the cliff you go,
E veryone has the right to shine.
A nyone can be free and belong.
M erriment everywhere you look,

W e don't bully, we are kind.
O nce a year, we celebrate differences,
R eunite every year and have
L ots of fun everywhere,
D o you want to come?

Isabelle Moore (9)
Mary Exton Primary School, Hitchin

Adventure

A dventure is calling me and my monkey
D oom might lie ahead but me and my monkey are not scared
V ivid flowers are scattered all around
E lephants I wish to ride... Oh wait, I'm already on one!
N ina is my toy monkey
T earing through the lush green of the forest
U sing my skills to get through the danger
R unning happily under a gushing waterfall
E nding on a high.

Elsie Moult (8)
Mary Exton Primary School, Hitchin

My Magical Dream

I open my eyes wide,
All I can see is the tide,
Confusion fills my mind,
A lovely lake drifting on the land and hugging the bushes,
I can only feel the pushes,
Of the whistling wind,
A beautiful unicorn bright and strong,
Singing a graceful song,
A rainbow blinding my eyes its vibrant colours never saying goodbye,
Where else would or could I find this perfection?
Hold on...
Is this just a dream?

Zara Bains (8)
Mary Exton Primary School, Hitchin

The Watcher's Gloomy Dream!

A cat hissing, a potion spilling,
A nightmare is coming upon me.
People called the Watchers watch me and my friends
Sleepover in my mansion.
Me sleeping in my secret room, with all my friends.
But then all of a sudden, the Watcher broke into my home
And me and my friends were running.
I fainted...
When I woke up, I was scared.
It was 3am. The creepy hour.
I was saying, "Please, help me!"

Lily-Mae Silman (8)
Mary Exton Primary School, Hitchin

The National Election

On a hot summer's day,
At the end of May,
The general election,
Is definitely not a reflection,
Of last year's.
When Boris Johnson gets all the votes,
Everyone falls into tears,
Well, not everyone, everyone except me,
Boris grabs a stabbing knife,
Sharper than a tee!
Chases us for our lives,
Catches up with us,
Until I found that that scream,
Was just a dream.

Sam Cook (8)
Mary Exton Primary School, Hitchin

Fortnite Millions Of Pounds

F ortnite, millions of pounds
O r be famous for playing Fortnite.
R ealising I have won the Fortnite World Cup.
T onight I am going on Fortnite.
N ow time to get on Fortnite.
I am the best Fortnite player ever.
T onight it is the Fortnite World Cup
E ase from the lobby.

Christian Collins (9)
Mary Exton Primary School, Hitchin

Dream Yum

D reaming sweets galore,
R unning on lemon sherbert,
E ven the door knocker is a candy cane,
A nd I can see popcorn,
M arzipan stools,

Y ummy sweet Wonder Land,
U nderestimating the amount of goodies,
M agnificent treats.

Verity Cahill (9)
Mary Exton Primary School, Hitchin

Rapper

R eally like rapping
A ll for rapping
P ushing my limits
P eople buying tickets
E ating, rapping to sing
R apping every day.

Henry Wilson-Dolan (8)
Mary Exton Primary School, Hitchin

Gloomy

G ravestones everywhere,
L onely,
O nly person is me,
O nly thing I see is fog,
M y heart is beating,
Y owling wolves.

Cleo Lewis (9)
Mary Exton Primary School, Hitchin

Dreams About Unicorns

I am in a dark place with my family,
But something starts to happen.
We start to fly, I fly very high in the sky.
There are lots of stars in the sky
And there is a rainbow.
On a unicorn, this is so fun!
I said my sisters are riding a unicorn too.
And my mummy and my mummy's partner.
"It's time to go home," said Mummy.
"Okay!" said my sister, but I didn't want to go home yet.
I hated to but I went.
This was a fun day, I said to my mummy, "Yes!"
The lot of us went home and on the way
I saw Storm so she went home with me.
She had a sleepover at my house
And it was so much fun!

Luna Johnson (8)
St Augustine's Catholic Voluntary Academy, Stamford

Dancing On The Moon

There are fairies dancing with other dancers,
They are dancing on the moon,
They also love running around,
They get lost with unicorns flying in the starry sky,
Magic falls from their wings,
Astronauts with me walking slowly,
I was with my friend Holly, as well,
We all feel calm with the clouds,
Dinosaurs go around in circles,
They look very happy,
We fly very high in the sky.

Lucy Milojevic (8)
St Augustine's Catholic Voluntary Academy, Stamford

The Wooden Mansion

When I fell asleep,
The first thing I saw was a bottomless pit,
I was with my family,
Including Tom, the cat,
Also Olivia,
Luna and Storm,
I looked around,
We were in the wooden mansion in the woods,
I felt like someone was watching me,
Then I saw lots of monsters,
And they surrounded me,
I noticed the bottomless pit surrounded me.

Talitha Randall-Carrick (8)
St Augustine's Catholic Voluntary Academy, Stamford

Benjamin's Flying Football Match

I can see some trees and leaves that look like me
I am with a flying footballer with superpowers
We are gliding to Benjamin's dreams
Excited and delighted to play football
But football gets interrupted by Benjamin
And his inflatable hammer that is cute
He bops it on to the stadium
He also has a demon called Dave.

Zachary Nye (7)
St Augustine's Catholic Voluntary Academy, Stamford

Once Upon A Dream

The spider had a poisonous bite,
Then, the unicorn and the fairy had an idea,
It was about to bite me,
I was in the spooky woods,
Then the spider jumped out on me,
I pushed him off me with a powerful blow,
From my fist,
The unicorn struck the spider and the spider hated it.

Olivia Atkinson (8)
St Augustine's Catholic Voluntary Academy, Stamford

Tom's Life

A spider has a dangerous power,
That power is webbing,
He webs around the busy city,
And he saves the city every day,
He is called Awesome Tom,
He has a massive lunch,
His lunch is cockroaches in milk,
The spider has super long legs,
And the spider is huge.

Tyler Downs (7)
St Augustine's Catholic Voluntary Academy, Stamford

Dream Land

D o you love others in your dream?
R uined when there is no love.
E qually when there is love and not.
A nd you are sometimes not in control of your dream.
M eans you might be mean or not.
S o go ahead and sleep.

Logan Brooks (7)
St Augustine's Catholic Voluntary Academy, Stamford

The Best Football Team

I was on a football pitch
The football pitch was very big
I was on the team of PSG
The best on the team I scored a goal
I loved PSG
Whilst I was playing football a rainbow distracted me
I fell over and my team lost.

David Sharp (7)
St Augustine's Catholic Voluntary Academy, Stamford

Sparkle Unicorn

A unicorn has a power and that is glitter everywhere
She loves to eat hay and grass
She is massive and her name is Emma
She loves to run around with her friends
She helps people in need.

Althea Penfold (8)
St Augustine's Catholic Voluntary Academy, Stamford

Space Unicorns

Space unicorns dance around my head
As I get ready for bed
I jump onto Luna unicorn
But I begin to yawn

Slowly I drift into pale blue misty skies
Space unicorns hop all around
They gallop, prance and pound
On fluffy pink marshmallow mounds

A sweet song fills my ears
A beautiful princess I see
Fearless and free
On clouds of raspberry cream
Pretty pink flowers and moonlight jewels

I stare at the beautiful sight
And take a big marshmallow bite
Suddenly, I'm awake!
Sitting in a giant purple bubbling lake.

Zoe Antao (8)
St George's Church Of England Foundation School, Broadstairs

Dino Dreams

D ay after day, I have dreams about ferocious dinos
or maybe they're terrifying nightmares
R emind me about the dreams I have and the one I
had last night
E xtraordinary things happened like dinos travelling
the world
A t bedtime I had a dream about a volcano erupting
which happened one night when everyone was
asleep... Then
M assive rivers of lava dripped from the volcano
S creaming for their lives dinos and people travelled
to the North Pole and soon after that I woke up and
realised it was all a dream.

Olly Page (9)
St George's Church Of England Foundation School, Broadstairs

The Good Old Wizard

I visited the famous wizard in Magic Town
He wore a purple gown
He was kind, but a bit grumpy
He asked me why I was there
With a trembling voice, I replied,
"I am here to learn magic!"
He gave a friendly smile
To my surprise, he said, "Come join me"
He taught me a special spell
To rescue people from trouble
Tried it on the cat
Which fell in the well
And it worked really well!

Nathan Prakash-George (9)
St George's Church Of England Foundation School, Broadstairs

Flying In The Wind

I watch the birds,
They fly so high,
Like they are dancing
In the sky.

Seeing the butterfly flutter
Without somewhere to go,
Is really rather special,
Like a little, floating bow.

In my dreams
I wish I could fly,
And glide through the sky,
Like a beautiful butterfly.

Marilyn Rae (9)
St George's Church Of England Foundation School, Broadstairs

Our Dream World

My dream is for the world clean and for love to fill our hearts,
For everyone's laughter, and to make orphans a son or daughter,
For littering to stop and also this bickering,
Pollution to go and more plants to grow.

Make the world a special place in our heart, as it's our clean world.

Matthew Caloudis (8)
St George's Church Of England Foundation School, Broadstairs

How I Discovered A Mummy

Golden statues here and there
In the corner, a child's chair
This chamber of secrets newly found,
A whole new universe away from the world
And then I see it on the floor,
A sarcophagus covered from head to toe in hieroglyphics
Who could want more?
And this is what I am pleased to say
What was inside blew me away!
I discovered a mummy
What happened next, I could not help
I woke up in my bed
No sarcophagus to be found.
I just woke up in the same old world.
But then I see it in the corner parts of my dream
Getting smaller and smaller.

Alba Barron (8)
St Hilary School, Goldsithney

Over The Ocean

The moonlight over the sea,
And the sunlight over the ocean,
Shining on the amazing creatures down there.
What a lot to explore!
Not just the fish, but the coral reefs, caves and submarine volcanoes
As well as those curious creatures

We have to look after our ocean,
So if you see any rubbish on the beach or in the water,
Pick it up and put it in the bin.
The ocean is precious with its waves and popping bubbles.
High above that wondrous ocean,
The rays of the sun lie quiet and still.

Alex Strong (8)
St Hilary School, Goldsithney

Life Is But A Dream

One day, when you sleep
You will find that you've gone too deep.
My breathing slows.
I could not ask for more.
To reach the end of the day-to-day bore.
As memories sift from hidden depths
I find myself in a tornado whirl.
Who is she? This mysterious girl?
Wrapped in a cloak of magic and swirl.
Her secrets she keeps close at hand.
A puzzle that we cannot understand.
In a wonderland, they lie hoping that they will die.
Forever drifting down the stream.
Life is but a dream.

Remé Weller (7)
St Hilary School, Goldsithney

TV Dreams

I was watching the TV
When something strange happened to me
I saw the show in 3D
I was in my favourite show,
How this happened, I don't know,
Who should I see coming from afar,
It was my favourite telly star!
We spent the day together,
We wanted to be best friends forever.
Then I felt a shake, and I was jolted awake,
I had made a big mistake
I was sitting in my chair,
With my teacher standing there!

Tilia Cholaj-Hickin (8)
St Hilary School, Goldsithney

The Future Of Our Oceans

I dream of the oceans and seas,
Being free of plastic and pollution,
No more Pacific garbage patch.

I dream of a kinder world,
With no large trawlers,
And no entangled animals.

I dream of colourful coral reefs,
No longer bleached,
More seagrass and kelp forests to support life,
And more protected areas in the sea.

I dream of the oceans and seas brimming with life.

Lowenna Hodges (7)
St Hilary School, Goldsithney

The Dream

Once I was getting ready for bed,
As soon as I closed my eyes,
I was in space,
I went through a black hole,
I was floating in space,
I saw some aliens,
They waved, so I had to wave back,
But I saw another black hole,
And randomly I appeared in the Atlantic Ocean,
I had to get out of there immediately,
But turns out I was on a humpback whale,
But when I woke up it was all a dream.

Esmae Cooke Maddern (8)
St Hilary School, Goldsithney

Monkey Planet

Monkeys are taking over the planet, oh no!
But never fear, Super Xander is here.
He takes them out with an almighty punch,
And wraps them up in a monkey bunch,

He throws them into outer space
Until next time, get out of this place.
The monkeys are gone, hip hip hooray!
So they have a celebratory parade.

Xander Smith (8)
St Hilary School, Goldsithney

Dragon Dreams

B edtime dreams, an egg with a crack.
A baby dragon inside with spikes on its back.
B ut it was whining consistently, non-stop.
Y ou want Mum? We set off with a hop.

D anger lurks at every turn.
R un little dragon, you have so much to learn!
A t the top of the hill, huge dragons flapped.
G usts making whirlwinds feels like we're trapped.
O h, dragons, oh dragons, look who is here.
N ice baby dragon, with no parents I fear.

R aising the baby up to the night sky.
E xtra intellect was gained by one that flew by.
T his mama dragon stopped at my feet.
U nsure what this meant, its breath filled with heat.
R oaring, calling for his mum.
N uzzling, cuddling, home he has come.
E nd is near, I fulfilled my quest.
D reams like these are the ones I like best!

Izabelle Skeef (11)
St Mary's Catholic Primary School, Bognor Regis

Princesses Have Feelings Too

There was once a princess locked up in a cold, tall tower.
One day, she wrote a poem about her feelings which went like this;
I can never be the one for anyone.
I can never find the one.
What is the one?
The one that loves you unconditionally.
The one that never says, "You need more make-up!"
The one that would protect you.
Do those exist out there?
Will they ever exist out there?
Do they exist only in my imagination?
My imagination is filled with rainbows, butterflies...
All a bit sad.
People tell me, "True love is hard to forget!"
But I still want to be protected and loved.
Why does he not exist?

Aleksandra Borisova (10)
St Mary's Catholic Primary School, Bognor Regis

The Food Escape

In the dead of night,
With no one in sight,
Except for the food escaping from the darkness to the light,
"So bright," said the Turkish Delight,
To the burger who just stared.

Over there, in the fridge,
Were the dates and the grapes,
So calm, it seemed my mistake,
"The fridge is going crazy,"
Said the burger to the Turkish Delight,
"Hide," he screamed, "before we all die!"

Meanwhile the pineapple was trying to battle the apple,
In the apple ring,
While the orange and pear sing,
They realised the alarm was about to ring,
They rushed inside and closed the door,
And people still wonder why food is so cold.

Edie Turner (9)
The Village Prep School, Belsize Park

I Dream

I dream of flowers blooming,
In every carpet of grass,
I dream of the sun shining,
In the cyan bright sky,
I dream of trees dancing,
Butterflies flying.

I dream of horses galloping,
Penguins painting,
I dream of ballerinas gracefully dancing,
Dogs playing.

I dream of bunnies hopping around,
Scrumptious chocolate coins that are to be found,
I dream of being as courageous as a lion,
Or as proud as a peacock.

I dream of family and friends, where they'll always be,
The Village School, the best school I have ever seen.

Seher Bhatia (9)
The Village Prep School, Belsize Park

The Dog

The dog is as brown as chocolate.
The dog is a cheetah.
The dog is as fluffy as a teddy.

The dog is thunder.
The dog is as late as the white rabbit in Alice in Wonderland.
The dog is a giant.

The dog is as sleepy as my mummy.
The dog is a statue.
The dog is as intelligent as me!

The dog is an elephant.
The dog is as sneaky as a mouse.
The dog is a shooting star!

The dog is as grumpy as my daddy.
The dog is a diamond.
The dog is as cool as Taylor Swift.

Sofia Lamani (9)
The Village Prep School, Belsize Park

Dreams

D izzying spells will be cast as quick as lightning.
R aging witches will spell.
E arthly fairies sparkle as bright as stars.
A ir pixies will make mischief.
M agic potion masters will steal.
S uch tricks they will do!

For in a world of dreams, these things do come true.

Clara Bluestone (10)
The Village Prep School, Belsize Park

Riding

R unning as fast as a cheetah
I n the earliest times in the morning
D reamer neighs as loud as a lion's roar
I feel the best feeling I have ever felt
N othing matters to me other than Dreamer, who
G allops into the sunrise, taking me with her.

Sadie Graber (9)
The Village Prep School, Belsize Park

Wonder

It's nine o'clock, time to relax,
My eyes start to doze off,
Peep, peep, peep, is all I hear,
As I fall off to dreamland,
My body slows down,
My worries disappear, as I go to my happy place,

I wake up on a poofy cloud and I run along with my pink cat Pearl,
I jump in the colourful flowers of oh so many palettes
Petals dance around me as I stare up at the sky,
I see a cloud that looks like a tiger but then I hear a noise,
I sit up and look around as it gets louder and louder,
I see trees and bushes and a small, little cat,
I tickle its chin and it bursts out with laughter,
It gives me a fright and I tumble down under,

I wake up in pools of sweat,
And I wonder, oh I wonder,
Was it my dream or an actual day of life?
Whatever it was, it was just a wonder.

Ava Johnson (11)
Warlingham Village Primary School, Warlingham

Nightmares

Nightmares crawl and nightmares creep,
They try to catch you in your sleep.
So when you think you're safe and sound,
They are watching you from all around.

When your heart fills up with dread,
And you twist and turn in your bed,
The nightmares laugh with evil glee,
They don't care for you and me.

They poison the dreams that fill our minds,
Those dreams become nightmares that start to unwind.
The nightmares are scary and fill us with fear,
We want them to leave us and just disappear.

But we have to wait until it comes to an end,
Nightmares are certainly nobody's friend.
Adults always say that it didn't happen,
So what really occurs when our eyelids blacken?

Are the nightmares always a part of the scheme,
Or is it really just a bad dream?

Charlotte Kinder (11)
Warlingham Village Primary School, Warlingham

The Fairies Of Wonder

Every night in my sleep,
I see the fairies as they leap,
Just around my moonlit floor,
I watched in awe as they opened my drawer,
I wondered what they could be getting out,
Was it a rubber or maybe a pencil?
Or perhaps my old handmade stencil,
Anyway, what they took,
I started to get more curious as I looked,
But then suddenly, one came over to me,
She told me her name and it was Jessie,
I started to question, why was she here,
And then her reply shocked me into tears,
She started to tell me, very quiet indeed,
That her mother was dead, and the last thing she touched was that pencil with lead,
But soon after that, it was time to go,
So I got up and opened the window,
As they were leaving, I stared at the sky,
I wonder if I should say goodbye.

Priya Gledhill (11)
Warlingham Village Primary School, Warlingham

Far Away Dreams

I wait for night to come, I'm very keen,
When the time has come I sit and dream,
What could I be this time?
A police officer fighting crime?
Or maybe a fearless fire-breathing dragon,
Could you imagine?

I could fly
Up high in the sky,
Or maybe I could be a pirate searching the seven seas,
Do you know how fun that could be?
I close my eyes, I squeeze them tight,
Excited for my adventurous night,

Oh, what could it be, I wonder,
I sit and wait and start to ponder,
Oh, what could it be?
Could I be part of royalty?
Night has come so I sit and lie,
What do you think I could be this time?

Grace McNally (10)
Warlingham Village Primary School, Warlingham

A New World

Out of the window, a world yet to find
Made up of a singular young mind
They put pen to paper
There could be nothing better
And now there is a new dimension
A true infestation
Of happiness, hopes and imagination
A place where dreams become reality
A place of great quality
A world that is surely meant to be
A world of a child's destiny
Through imagination's lens, the world floats off the page
Through reality's lens, they seemed to be caged
They dive inside
A world where they can thrive
They're in a book!
Come and take a look!
A world of pure elation
Do you have imagination?

Christiana Haridimou (11)
Warlingham Village Primary School, Warlingham

Dogs, Dragons And Dinosaurs

Dogs, dragons and dinosaurs don't usually make good friends.
But in my dream last night, they decided to climb Big Ben.
They were in a race to the top before the clock struck ten,
But as the bell chimed, they all fell down again.

When they got back home, they were all in a sob,
They hurt their hands, they hurt their knees, and their hairy heads.
Their mums were cross with their games
So they put them all to bed.
Their mums told them to play other games
Which were much more suitable for them instead.

They learned their lesson well,
They learned not to climb a giant clock with a giant bell!

Gracie Solanki (11)
Warlingham Village Primary School, Warlingham

Gymnastics Fantasy

When I'm asleep, I dream big
When I'm awake, I dream big
My biggest dream is gymnastics
My coach always says
'Jump off the beam
Flip off the bars
Follow your dreams
And reach for the stars'
Nothing can get me down
I will never frown
But as long as I can dream
Gymnastics is always the theme.

Isabella Willmott (10)
Warlingham Village Primary School, Warlingham

Violet

There was a dragon called Violet
She lived in a cold climate,
There she stayed as seasons went by
Violet could fly with powers coming to life,
She caused all the strife
Trouble gave her delight,
All through the night
Her purple scales
Shone through strong gales,
If you ever meet her she won't stay long
It would all seem so wrong.

Chloe Finch (10)
Warlingham Village Primary School, Warlingham

Fantastical Creatures

Once upon a dream, I wake up,
A fire gleams in my face.
Shadows slither towards me like snakes,
I don't believe this is a dream.

I dash to my window to see
A dragon roaring over my head.
Inside, I feel a shiver up my spine
And a bit of dread.
I don't believe this is a dream.

Centaurs making loud thuds
As they chase the roaring wind.
I see griffins soaring
In and out of trees.
I don't believe this is a dream.

A griffin approaches me out of the gloom,
I feel as happy as when I see blossoms bloom.
I don't believe this is a dream.

But then, darkness falls.
I feel scared, dead,
I don't believe this is a dream.

The griffin darts away,
I run after him, I find him stone-cold,
Lying dead on the hard ground.
I don't believe this is a dream.

Then I wake up in my warm, cosy bed.
The sunlight illuminates my mythical creatures.
I do believe that was a dream!

Ben Maye (10)
West Chiltington Community School, West Chiltington

An Undiscovered Creature

Once upon a dream, when I lay my head to go to bed,
I dream of an ocean as huge as can be,
A sea as blue as the sky,
Once upon a dream, below diving dolphins,
Below the rushing waves, is a unicorn of the sea,
A creature as stunning as a summer day,
Once upon a dream, under singing whales,
Under this surface, by a beach,
Is an underwater creature with two fins,
A tusk and a waggly tail,
Once upon a dream, lies a mythical creature undiscovered,
Is this a dream? Am I awake?
A wonderful creature, a creature of beauty,
What is this creature?
It has an incredible feature,
Fragile fins, a trembling tail and a tempting tusk,
Half whale, half unicorn,
Yes, a unicorn of the sea,
As I wish this moment could last forever,
I'm as happy as one could ever be,
Once upon a dream.

Amber Joyce (9)
West Chiltington Community School, West Chiltington

Space Dream

S tepping from planet to planet like a tumbling gymnast,
P ointing at stars, counting them one by one,
A bove Earth, I float while dipping down like a soft cloud,
C olonies of stars shine over me as bright as the sun,
E verything is black and dark; there's no light, no brightness,

D ustings of stars cover the planets' beauty,
R unning across the rings of Saturn like a sprinter,
E xtraordinary colours that you would never see on Earth,
A mazing! Wow, I can see the United States' flag on the moon,
M y tired eyes begin to shut and I fall below, down to a cosy, fleecy cloud; I drift off to sleep.

Jazmine Simmons (9)
West Chiltington Community School, West Chiltington

The Dream...

Once upon a dream, I thought I woke up,
A house as empty as a blank sheet of paper.
A garden as lifeless as an empty paved street,
No one there apart from me.
I walked downstairs, opened the front door,
I discovered much, much more.
Glistening lakes, mermaids swimming,
Lush green trees, centaurs building,
Clear blue sky, griffins soaring.
I ran out into the area, happiness winning,
Griffins fell, sky darkening,
Centaurs screamed and ran leaving their builds,
Mermaids drowned, no longer swimming.
Trees fell, into the clearing,
Lakes drained, into the dirt,
Sky went grey, rain started pouring.
Sadness had won, I really was alone.

Rafferty Helms-North (10)
West Chiltington Community School, West Chiltington

In My Dreams...

In my dreams every night,
Waters swish across my long, slippery legs as I glide deeper into my clear turquoise waters.

In my dreams every night,
The sun beams through silky tops of glamorous oceans, gently hitting my arms with whirling whispers of shine.

In my dreams every night,
I see gorgeous corals gleam, amber, aqua and cream.
These are the colours that are standing out at the bottom of the ocean while creatures glide above their beam.

In my dreams every night,
Creatures in this ocean of mine, will glide across slippery seaweed strands which sway in the ocean's elegant movements.

This has to be a dream...
Right?

Esme Ackroyd (10)
West Chiltington Community School, West Chiltington

Once Upon A Dream...

Once upon a dream, rolling rivers ran and lush, silky willow trees lurched over me as a sad mood glided across the breeze.
Once upon a dream gorgeous flowers bloomed, cherry blossoms on the ground, the smell of juicy fruits filled the air.
Once upon a dream, fire-coloured leaves crisp under my numb feet, my nose cold and cheeks pink.
Once upon a dream, graceful snow gently fell, rocking itself to sleep, the smell of cosy hot chocolate spread across the air.
Once upon a dream, moonlight shone through curtains above my head, I woke up again to my soft bed.

Juno Hammond Russel (9)
West Chiltington Community School, West Chiltington

Mystical Forest

Once upon a dream, a blurry image, colour exploding
through the blossom trees dancing in the sunlight,
I do not believe this is a dream.
Booming footsteps in the distance, ground shakes like
a boat in a violent storm,
I do not believe this is a dream.
A group of towering centaurs gallop past, the remains
of their colossal footsteps making marks in the mud.
All I hear are flies buzzing away and wind raiding my
face,
I do not believe this is a dream.
I look around in amazement at my stunning
surroundings.
Once... upon... a... dream...

Lucas Hirsch (9)
West Chiltington Community School, West Chiltington

Airport Of Infinity

As I close my eyes, a world comes into view,
With an airport of new,
Planes like monsters fly over my head,
People work together like bees in a hive,
Planes from every country come to rest here,
In an airport of infinity,
As I imagine the flight ahead,
Sunlight runs across my head,
As I walk I feel the rush,
Just as I wonder about the flight ahead,
In an airport of infinity,
As my plane comes into view,
Everyone can't wait for the new,
Once upon a dream, I'm in an airport of infinity.

Ethan Zuanella (9)
West Chiltington Community School, West Chiltington

My Magical Sea Dream

In my underwater dream, the warm sea sparkles.
While friendly dolphins leap like ballerinas.
The eels slither like snakes.
While the colourful clownfish glide like dolphins.
Crabs crunch noisily on the salty sand.
While slippery stingrays brush against me.
The magical sea turtles swim through the warm, turquoise sea.
The starfish sparkle brightly on the old grey rocks like diamonds.
Octopuses twist and turn through the clear water like leaves twisting and turning in the air.

Lily Pannell (10)
West Chiltington Community School, West Chiltington

The Bay

Down by the bay,
Where the watermelons rot,
There is a lake,
That runs like it's awake,
With weeds that thrive,
And lush trees that rise,
With fish that flinch,
And ants that sprint,
Flowers that dance,
Leaves that prance,
Sloths that laze,
As I gaze,
At the navy blue sky,
I start to ponder,
I awake in my pale pink bed,
And rest my tired head,
Hoping I go back to the bay.

Dellilah Cox (9)
West Chiltington Community School, West Chiltington

My Enchanted Dream Ocean

Once upon a dream,
I dive into my enchanted world
With mythical creatures.
Seaweed dances like ballerinas,
Tiny little stripy fish glide through the lush grass.
Pink dolphins leap in the shape of a bright rainbow.
The sea is as blue as a bubblegum ice cream.
This world is a dream of hope and joy.
The sand is like a silk pillow
At the bottom of the ocean.
And then I wake up
And realise it was a dream.

Isabella Zalesny (9)
West Chiltington Community School, West Chiltington

Candyland Dreams

In Candyland, big, fluffy marshmallows jump up and down on the soft sweet ground.
Candyfloss is as fluffy as soft, silky clouds.
As I lie in bed, the marshlight shines in my room, illuminating the compact, scrunched-up sweet wrappers.
As I walk out of my cosy, secure house, ginormous marshmallows leap like frogs.
Yucky sour sweets make your eyes water.
I strain to wake up to get back to my comfortable bed.
What an adventure.

Jesse Strutton (9)
West Chiltington Community School, West Chiltington

Enchanted Fun

In my magical dreams every night.
A spark of enchantment hits me in my dream.
Fairies spin and flip like graceful ballerinas.
The trees swish about all silky like a blooming spring flower.
Pixies laugh cheerfully with berry juice over their faces.
A pixie pulls me to play, we leap and jump.
It's time for my dream to end.
I wave goodbye, oh what fun we have had.
And now I am here, lying in my bed.

Daisy-Mai Don (9)
West Chiltington Community School, West Chiltington

The Enchanted World

Once upon a dream,
I lie down in my soft bed,
I close my sleepy eyes,
Waiting for an amazing surprise,
I wake up with a fright,
A magical world starts to light,
Trees dancing like a break dancer,
There are animals everywhere,
I hear movement,
A whoosh comes right over my head,
It's a black, fire-breathing dragon,
As I touch it, I awaken in the real world,
Once upon a dream...

Freddie Overton (9)
West Chiltington Community School, West Chiltington

My Golden Hour

As I lie on my luxurious bed,
I rest my tired head,
I close my sleepy eyes,
Suddenly, I wake with a surprise,
Right in front of me,
What do I see?
A huge candy castle where gummy bears boogie,
Look to the left then to the right,
See this wonder world come to life,
Walking over to the soft, squishy marshmallows,
I give them a try,
Whoah! They bounce me high,
Our golden hour is nearly up,
One thing before we go,
Once
Upon
A dream.

Jake Paradise (9)
West Chiltington Community School, West Chiltington

Bouncing Clouds

As I lie in the darkness a light
Illuminates my huge squashy cloud plushy,
I fall asleep, my dream is about
Lush clouds hovering above the warm open sky,
As they bounce around getting immense,
Then minutes, watching them rain into the tropical teal ocean below,
As they form into mystical animals, objects and more.
Sharply, I wake up,
What an amazing dream that was.

Thomas Roberts (10)
West Chiltington Community School, West Chiltington

The Glittering Mountains

Mountains are as white as glittering stars.
Our tent is cloaked in paper-like snow.
Under the blue ice, my mum and dad take a cold dip.
Now I eat a nice warm fish I caught yesterday.
Imagine the air so fresh and the sky so blue.
No place could be like this.
Suddenly, I wake up and find I was dreaming, but I would definitely have this one again for sure.

Lara Budd (10)
West Chiltington Community School, West Chiltington

The Luscious Ocean Dream

Once upon a dream,
I wake up in a glassy ocean,
Shining like a rainbow vase
In my underwater dream,
I am a fantastic scuba diver
Exploring the waters,
A joyful, colourful, prickly octopus,
Swirls like a DJ in their reflection
The schools of fish swim around
The bright coral reef like squished raindrops,
When I have my extraordinary lucky dream
Suddenly, my eyes open until the end.

Dulcie Jessup (9)
West Chiltington Community School, West Chiltington

A Cold Dream

We tread, *crunch, crunch,*
Hear shuffles of the leaves beneath the snow.
Branches sway in the cold wind,
While heaving off vast icicles, as blue as the ocean.
We see several white bunnies the size of snowballs,
Bouncing across the field of snow and ice.

Bria Urquhart (10)
West Chiltington Community School, West Chiltington

YoungWriters Est. 1991

YOUNG WRITERS INFORMATION

We hope you have enjoyed reading this book – and that you will continue to in the coming years.

If you're a young writer who enjoys reading and creative writing, or the parent of an enthusiastic poet or story writer, do visit our website **www.youngwriters.co.uk**. Here you will find free competitions, workshops and games, as well as recommended reads, a poetry glossary and our blog.

If you would like to order further copies of this book, or any of our other titles, then please give us a call or visit **www.youngwriters.co.uk**.

Young Writers
Remus House
Coltsfoot Drive
Peterborough
PE2 9BF
(01733) 890066
info@youngwriters.co.uk

YoungWritersUK **YoungWritersCW**
youngwriterscw **youngwriterscw**